Some of the Adorable Dogs that can be found Inside

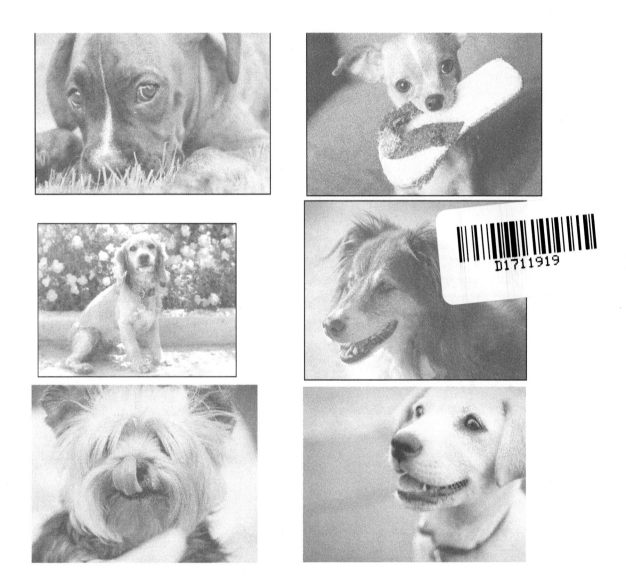

Visit my website at http://www.coffeeandcoloring.com

View my Etsy shop at http://www.artbyericah.etsy.com

Like my page on Facebook http://www.facebook.com/coffeeandcoloring

Tutorials at http://www.youtube.com/c/ericahenrycolors

Hi there. My name is Erica Henry and I am the creator of *Gray to Gorgeous* adult coloring book series. I'm so glad that you decided to purchase a copy of my book. I have spent hours and hours finding these adorable photographs and getting them ready for you to grab your art supplies and turn them into your own creations.

Coloring a grayscale photograph can be intimidating at first but just let your creativity flow and follow the natural highlights and shadows within the photograph. The photograph has done all of the hard work of figuring out where lights and darks should go, use it as a guide to bring the photograph to life.

If you would like to watch a tutorial on how to color grayscale images go to: https://youtu.be/mAGjCtbhMYo

I have included some blank pages in this book so you can take them out and use them as a protection page as a precautionary measure to prevent bleed through when using markers or gel pens.

Please visit my website at http://www.coffeeandcoloring.com and say hi. I also have tutorials there as well. I love to see your coloring pages that you've done so please post them to Facebook page http://www.facebook.com/coffeeandcoloring.

I hope you are as excited to start this coloring journey, as I was to create the book. Now, grab your coloring supplies and get to coloring

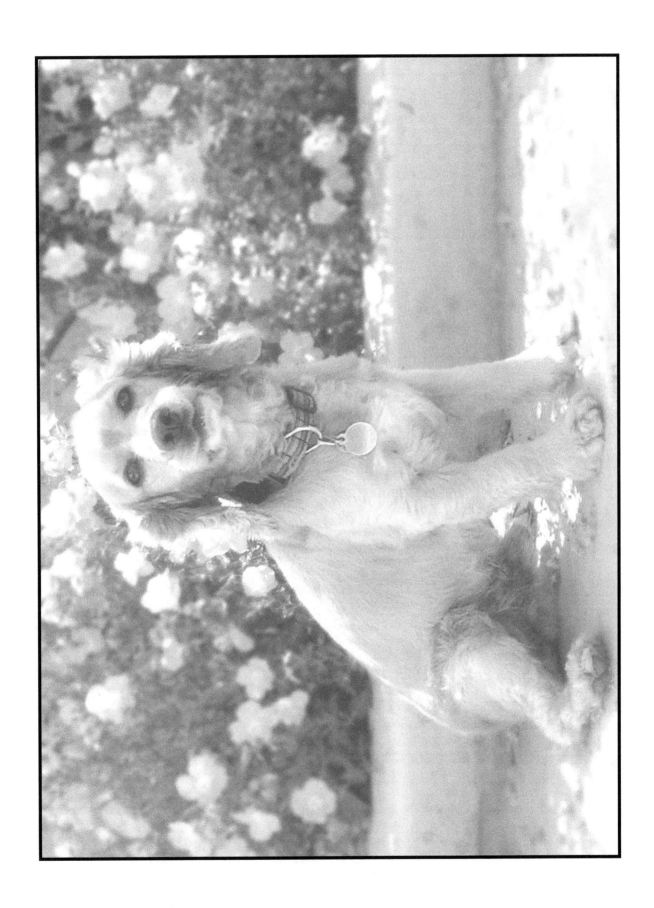

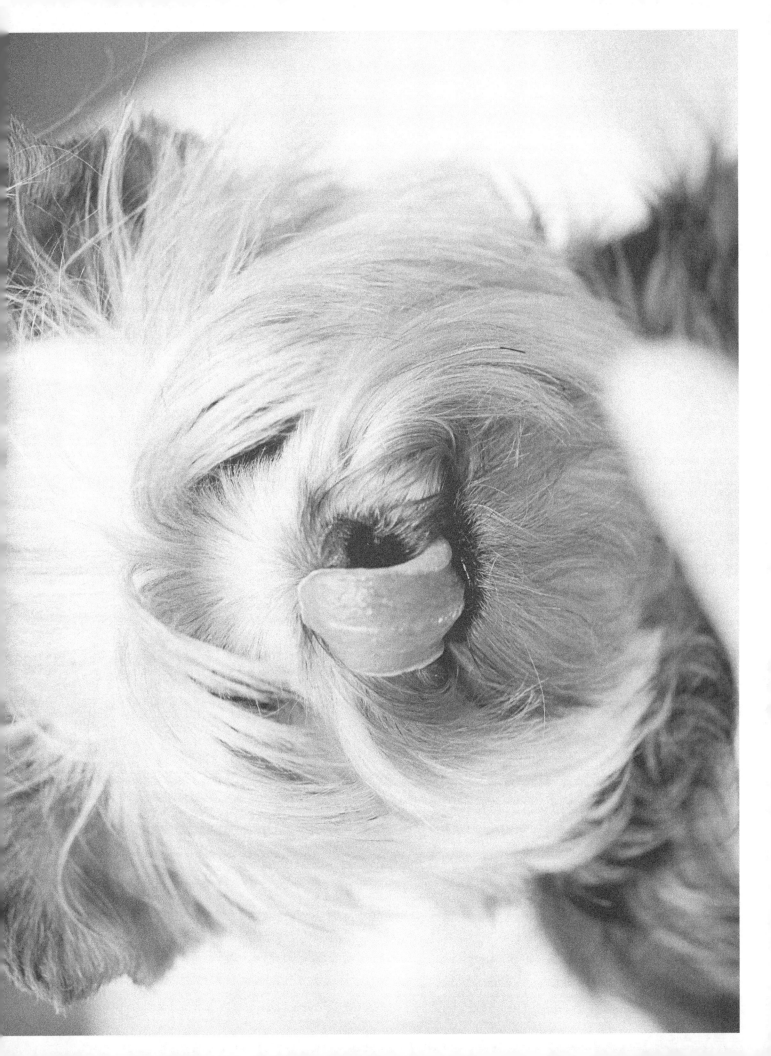

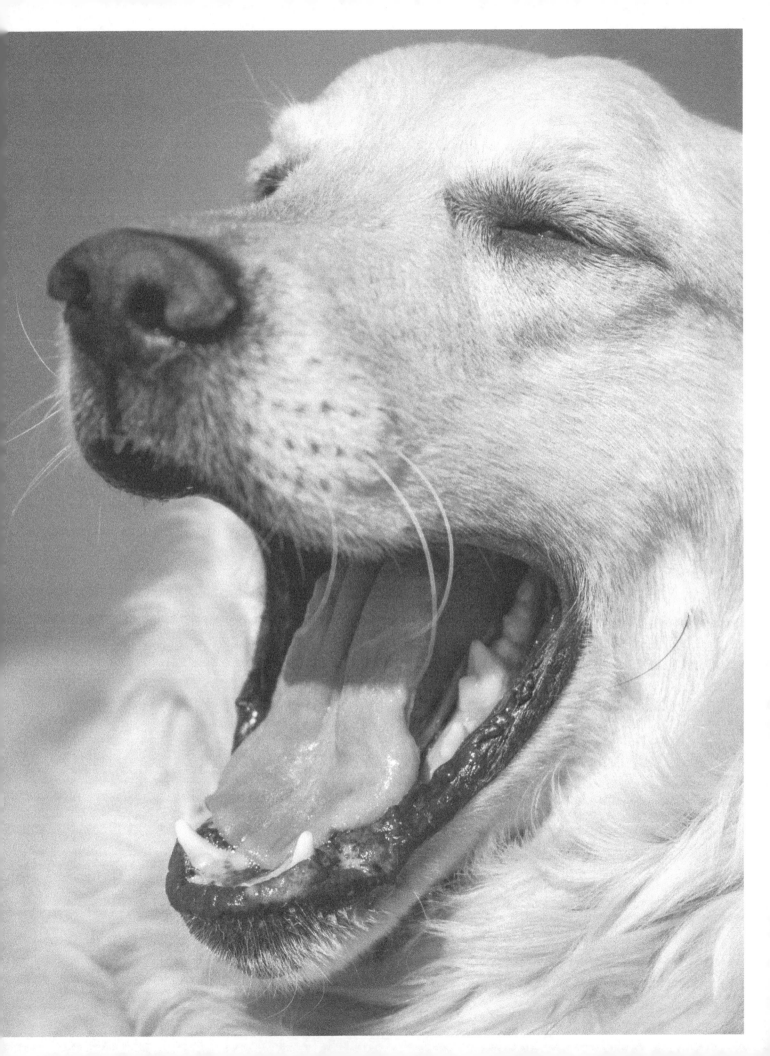

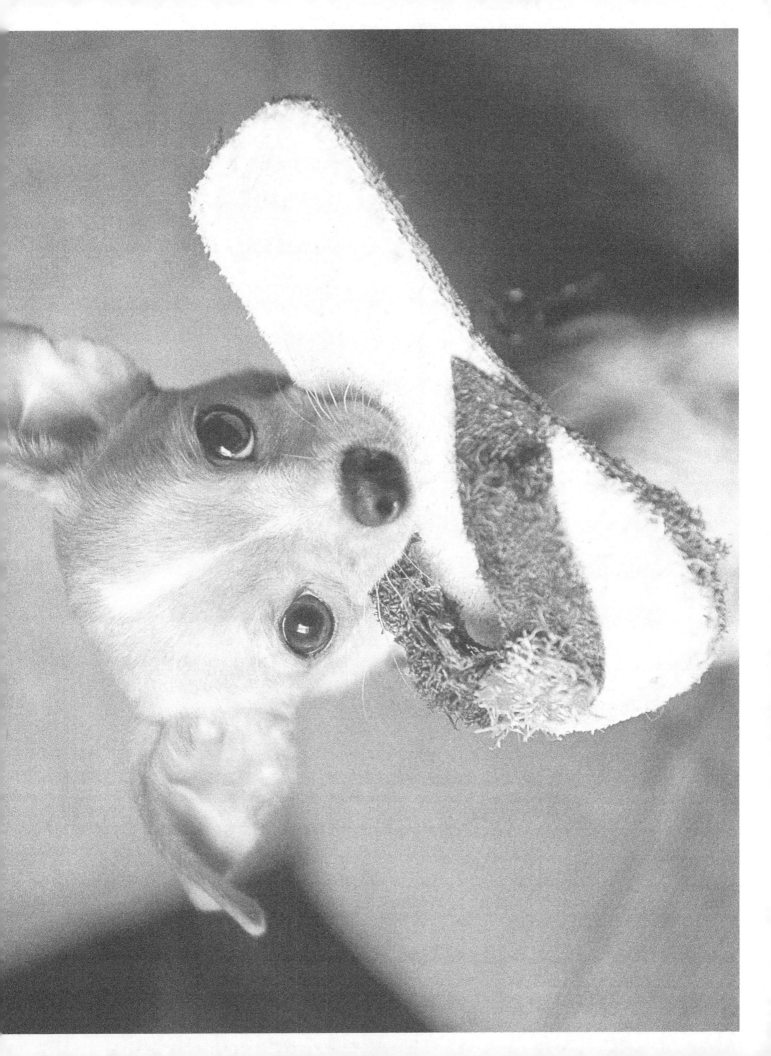

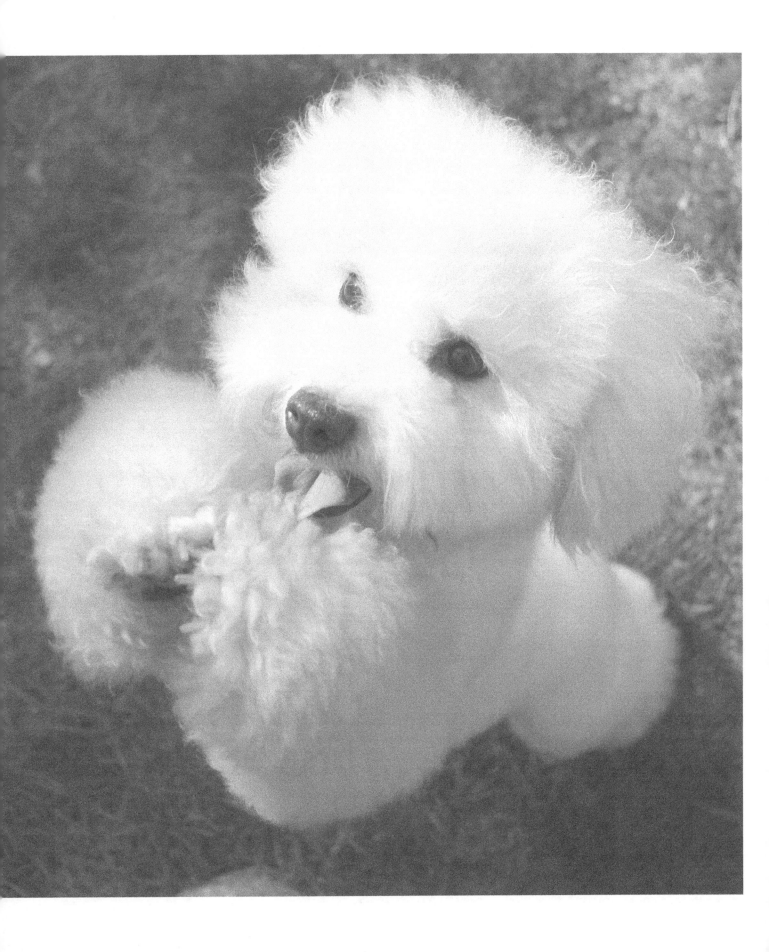

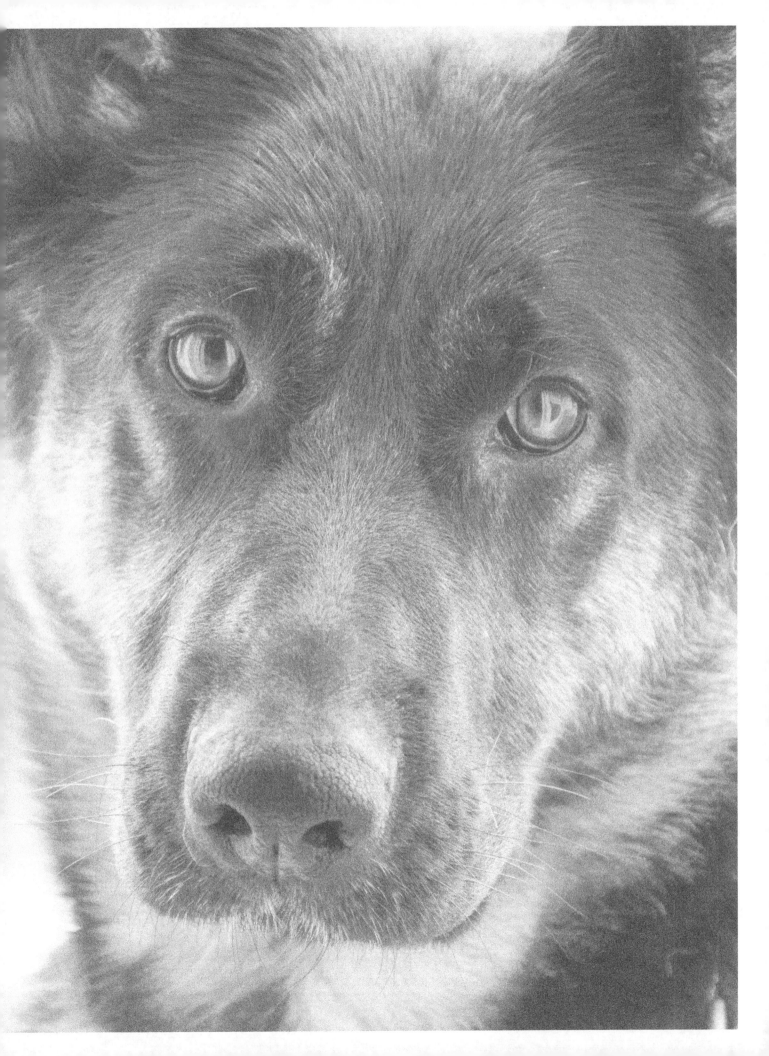

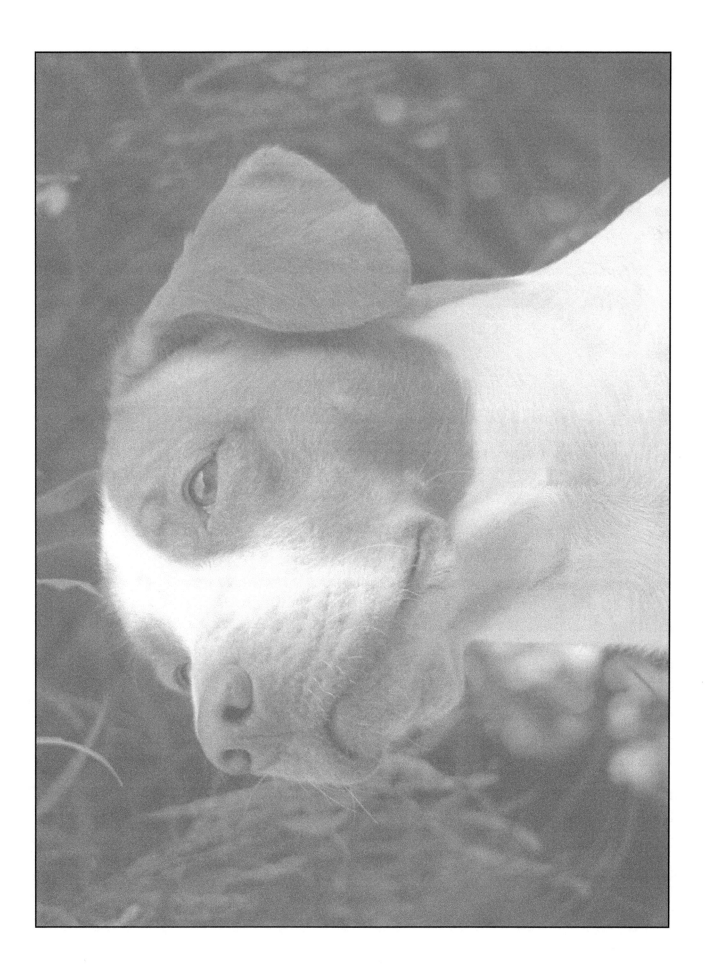

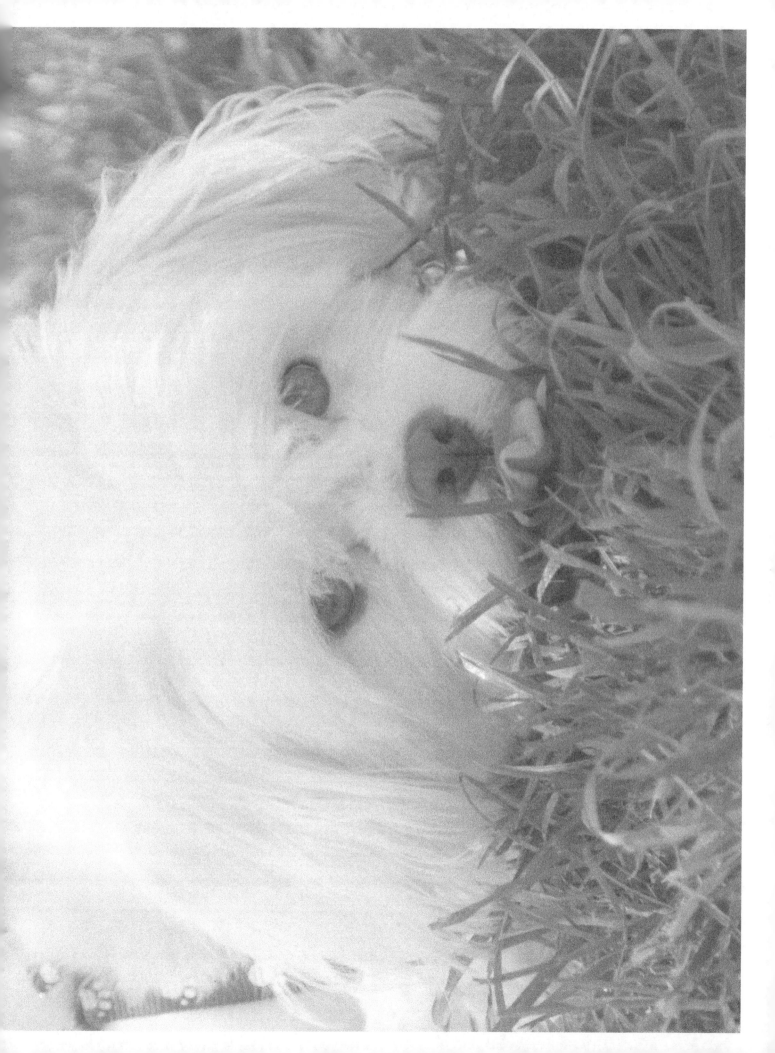

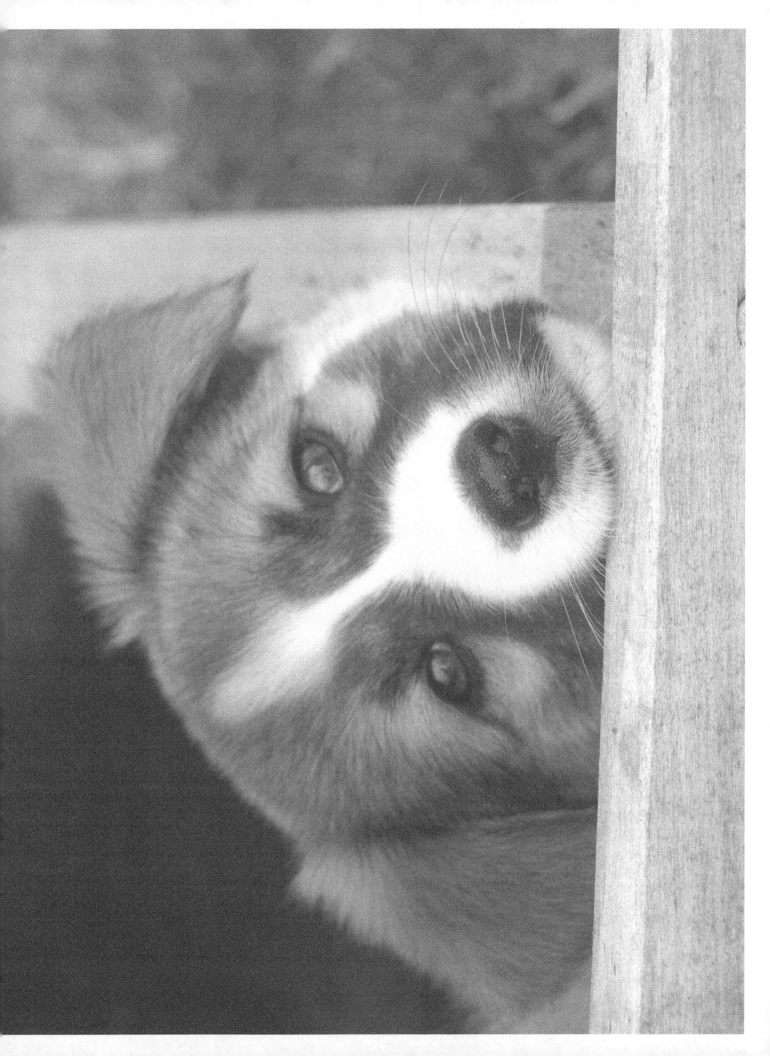

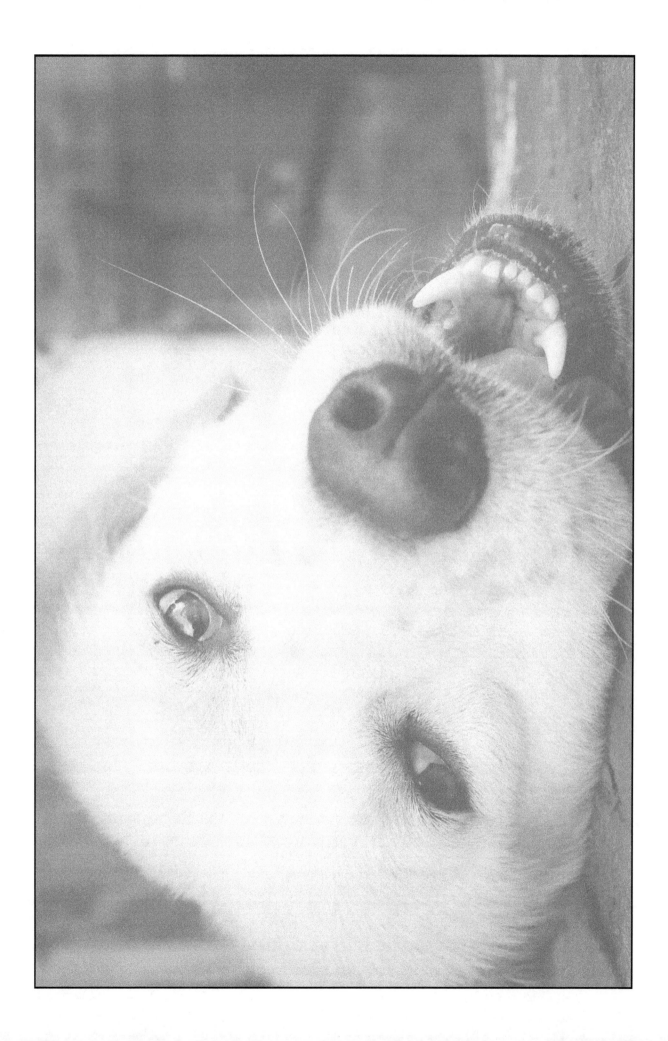

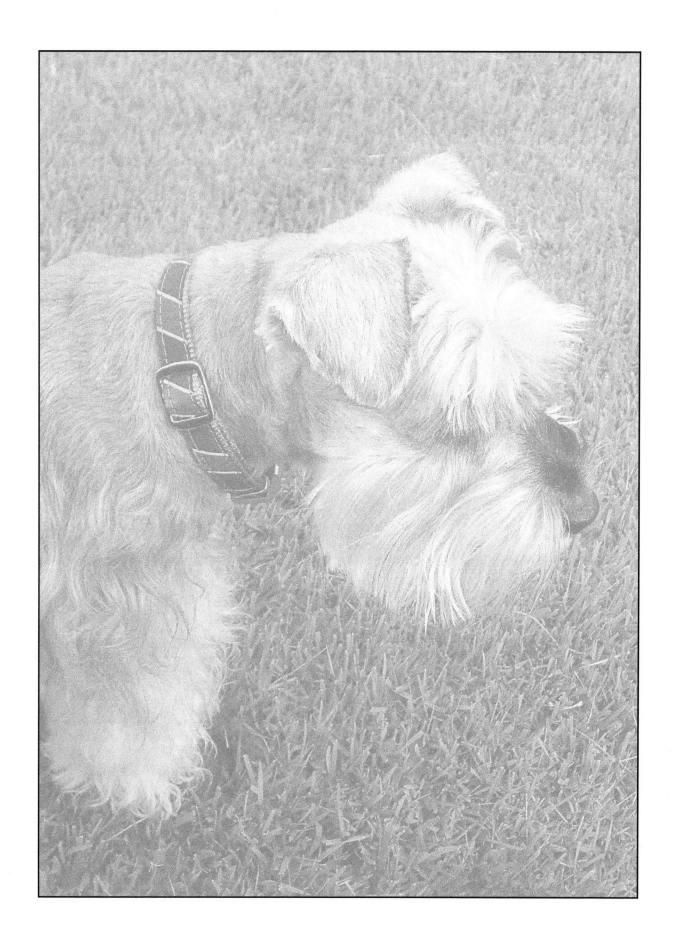

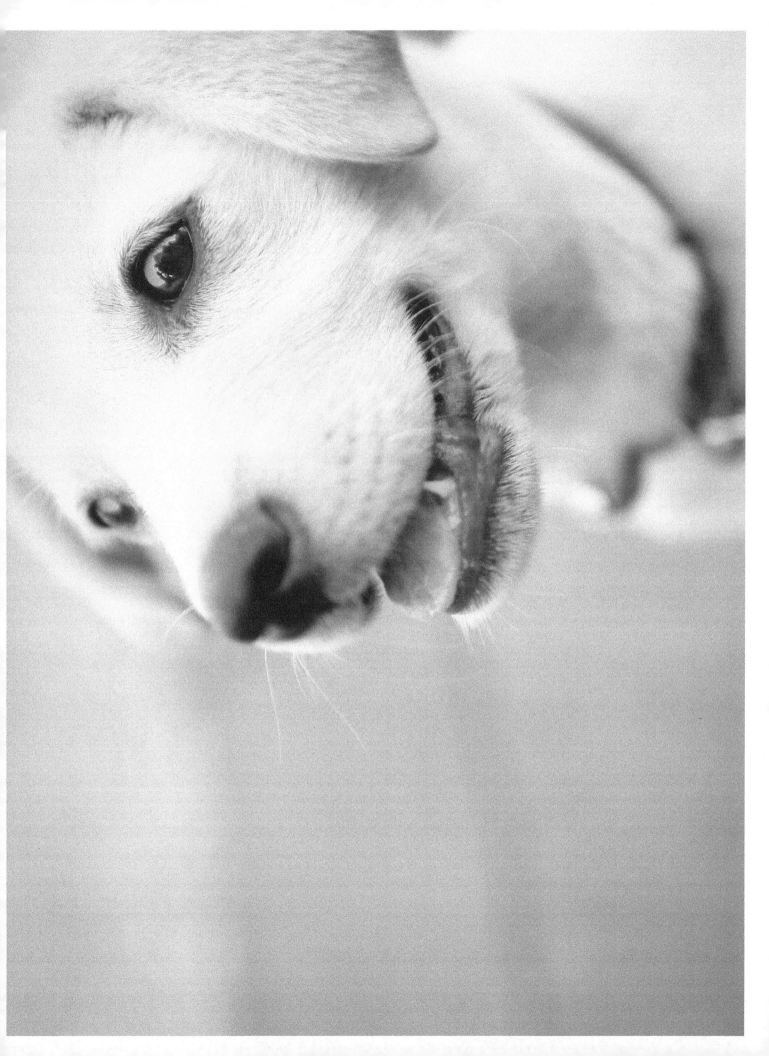

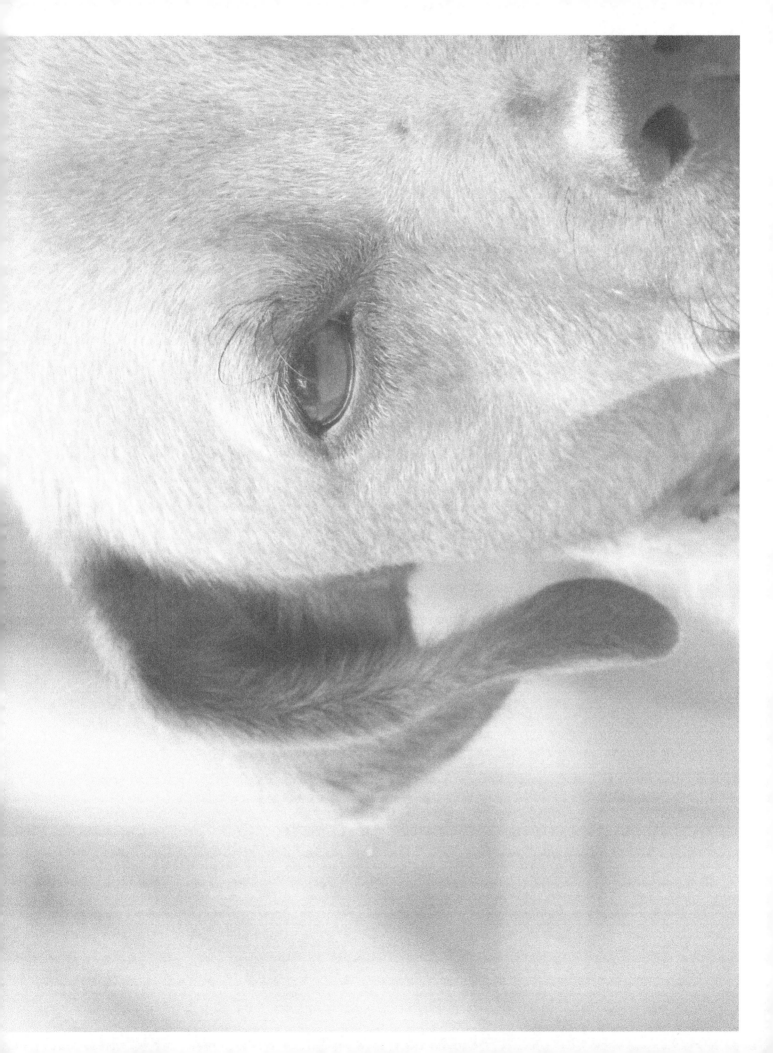

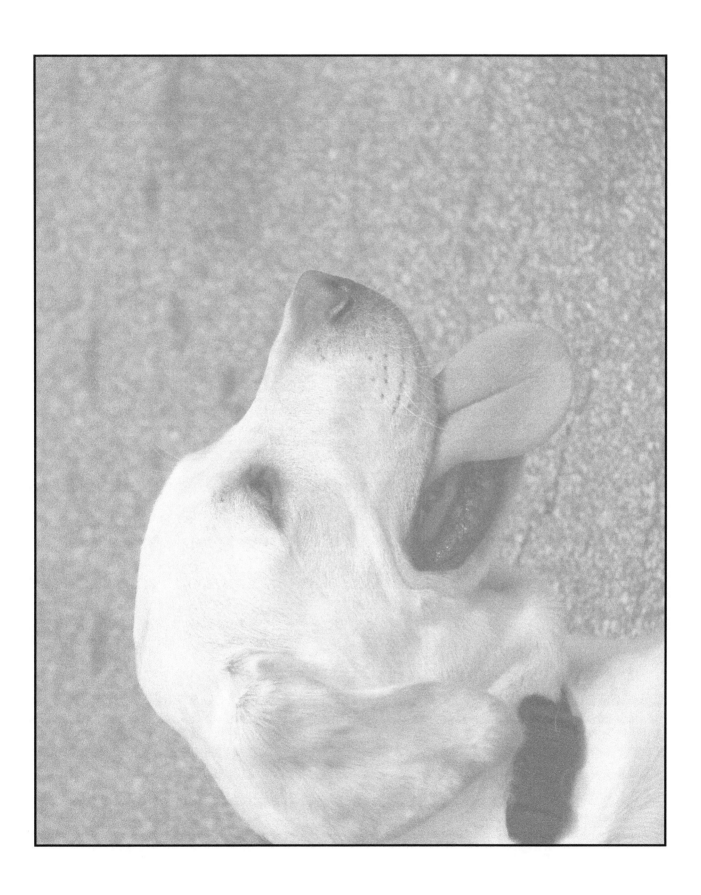

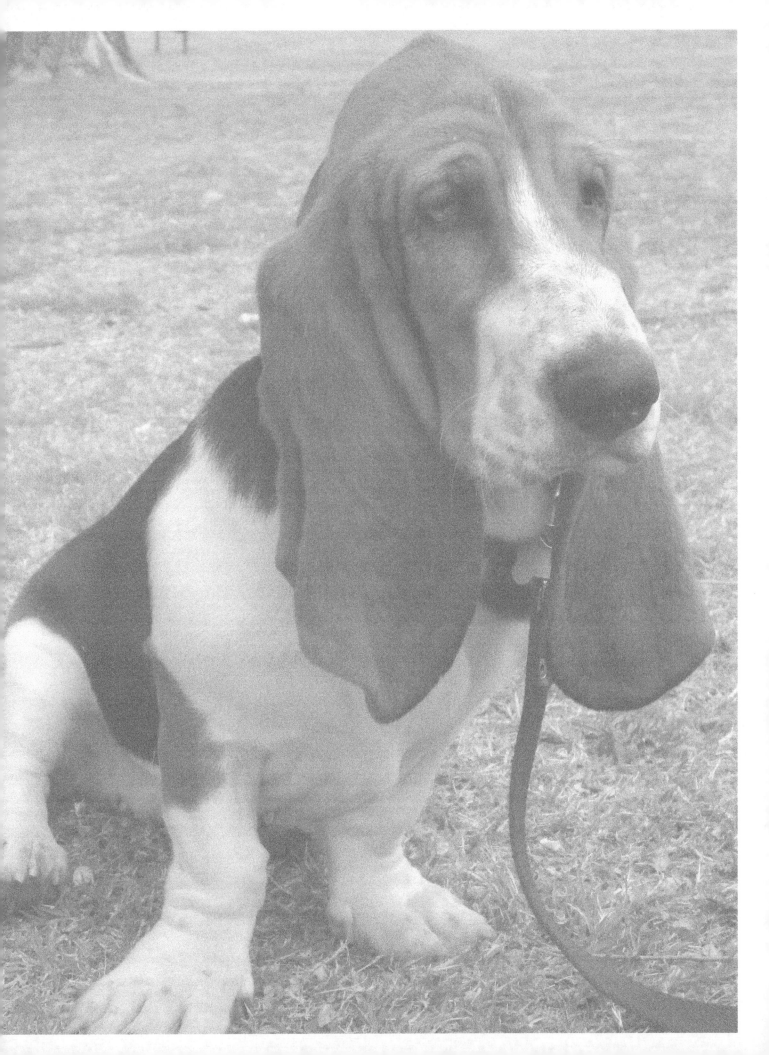

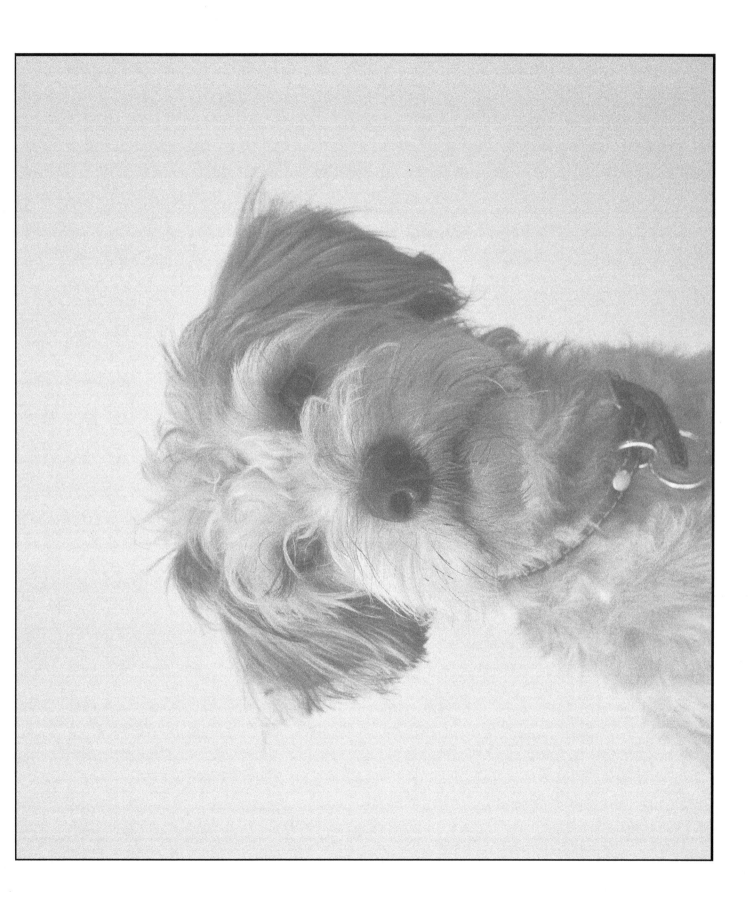

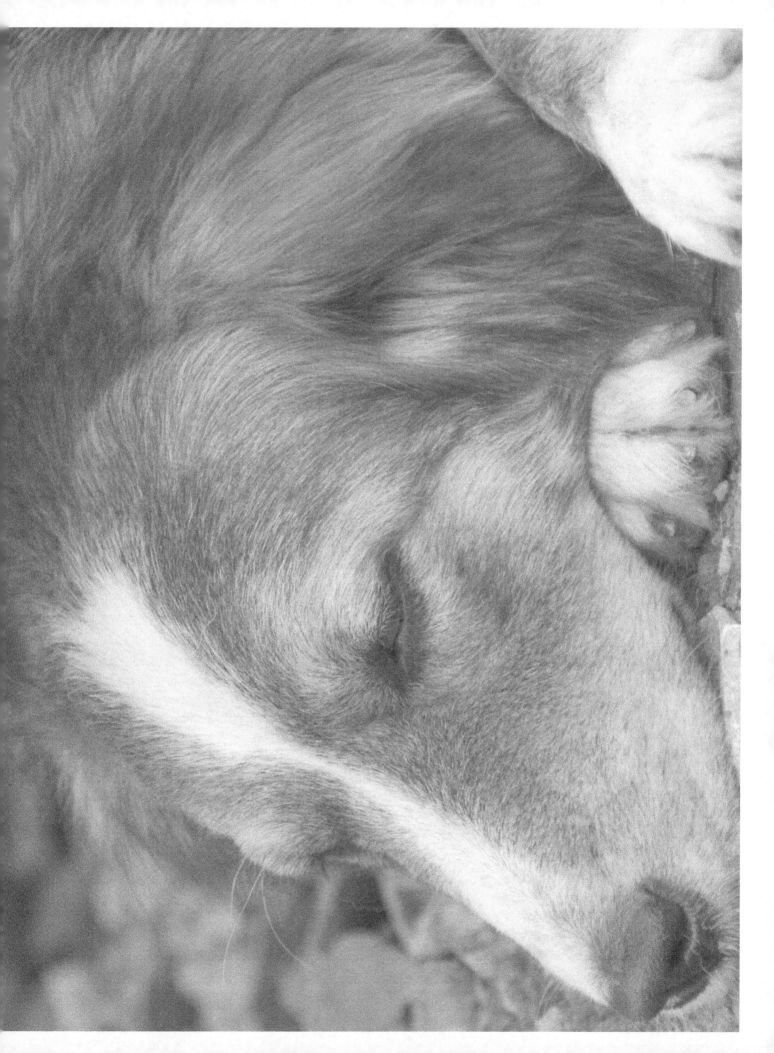

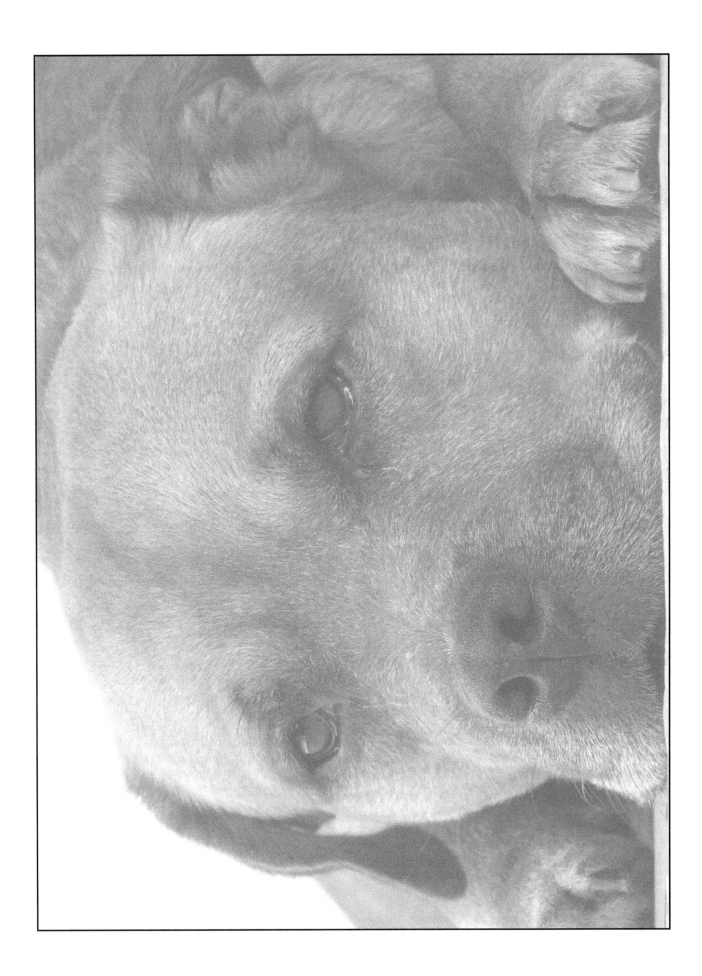

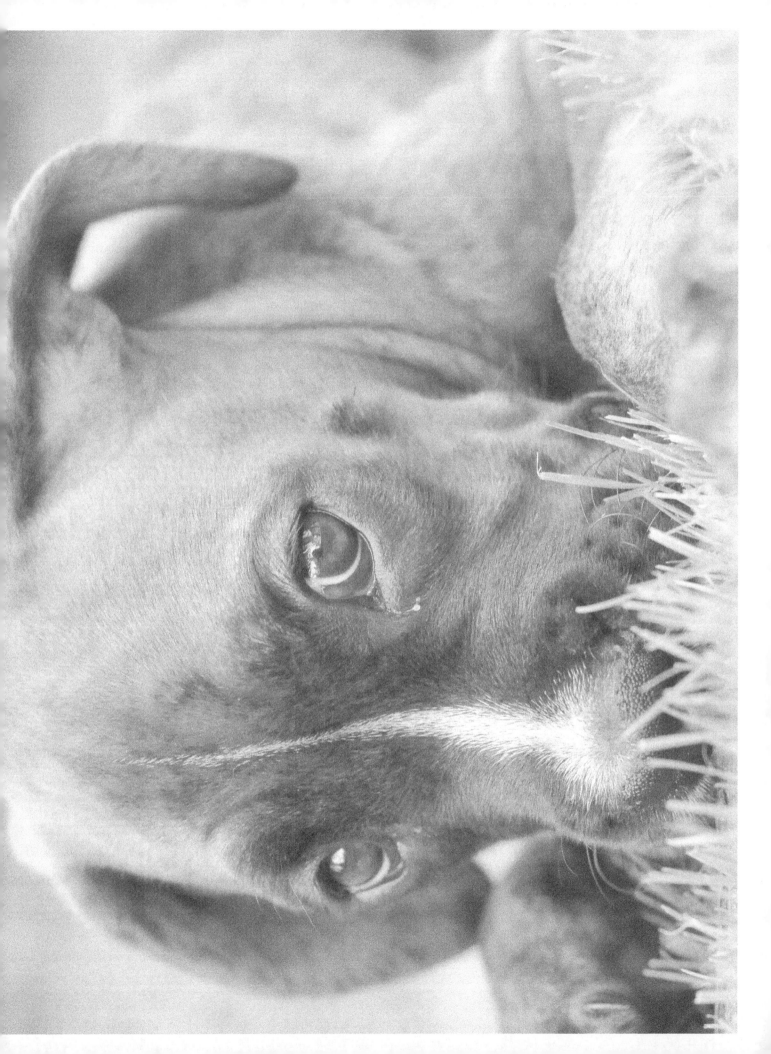

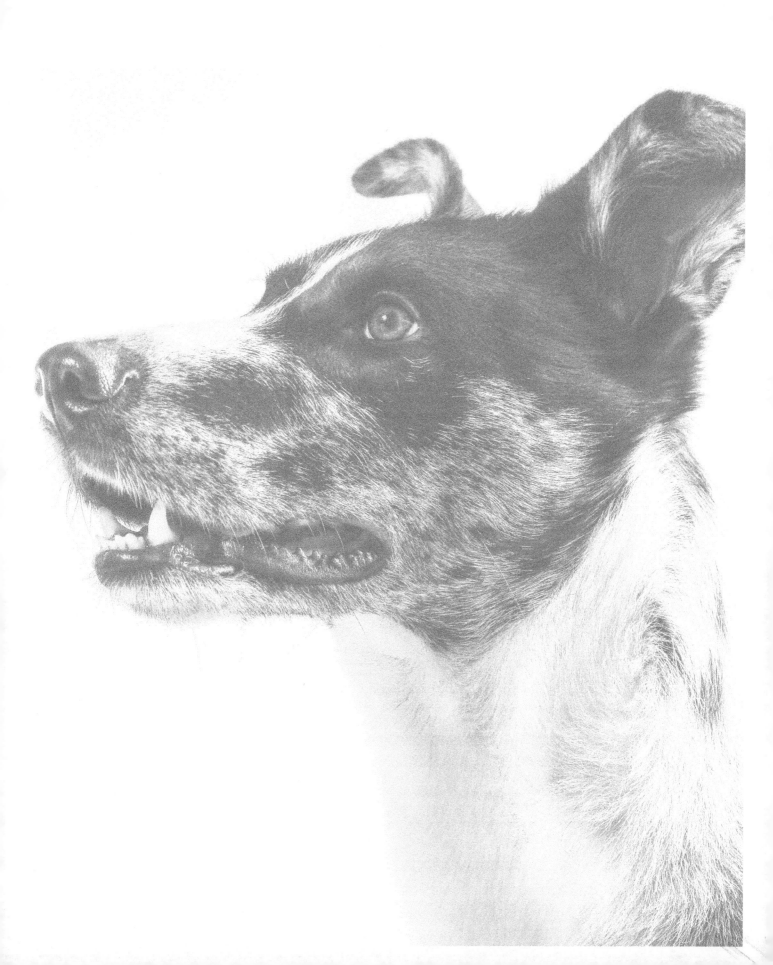

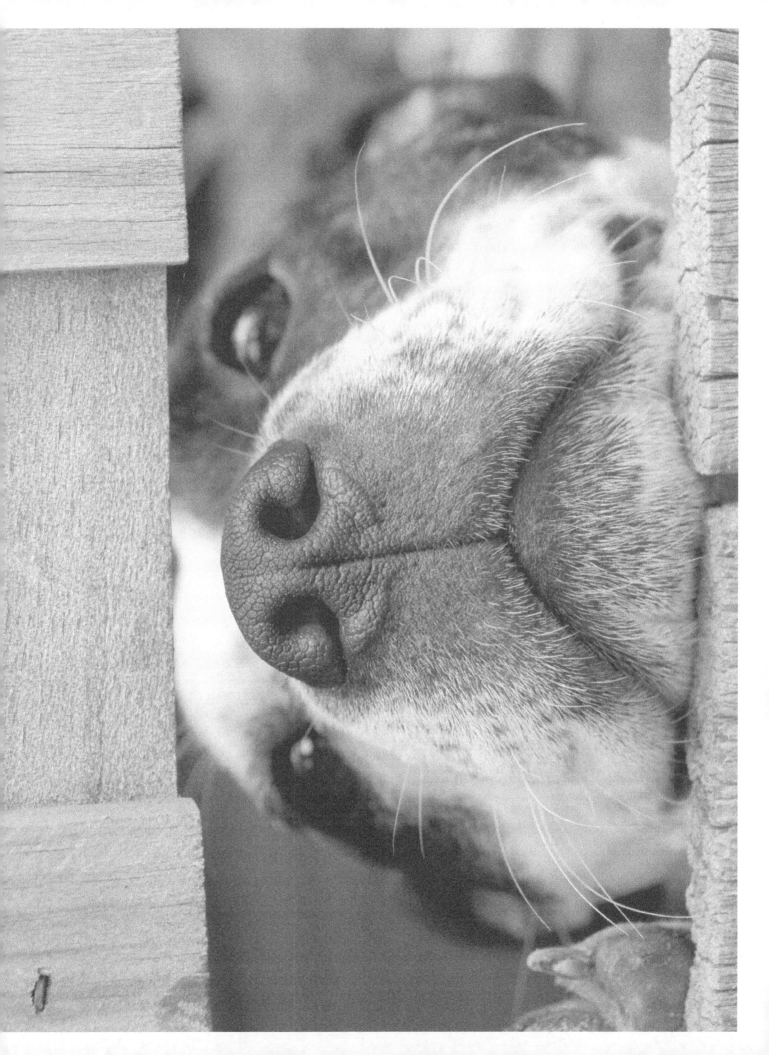

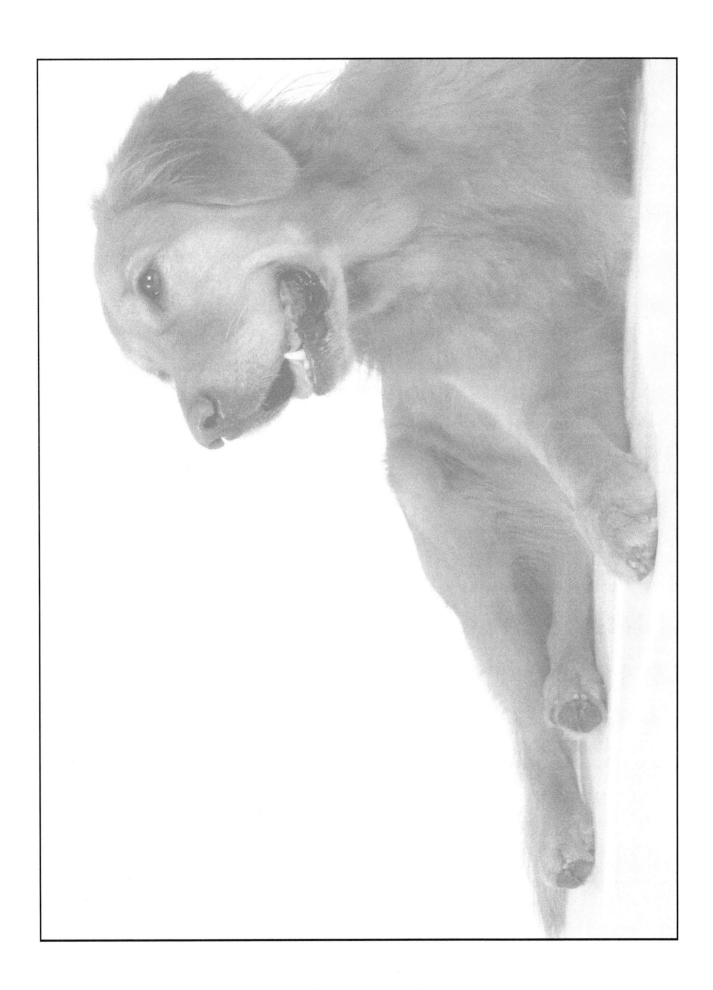

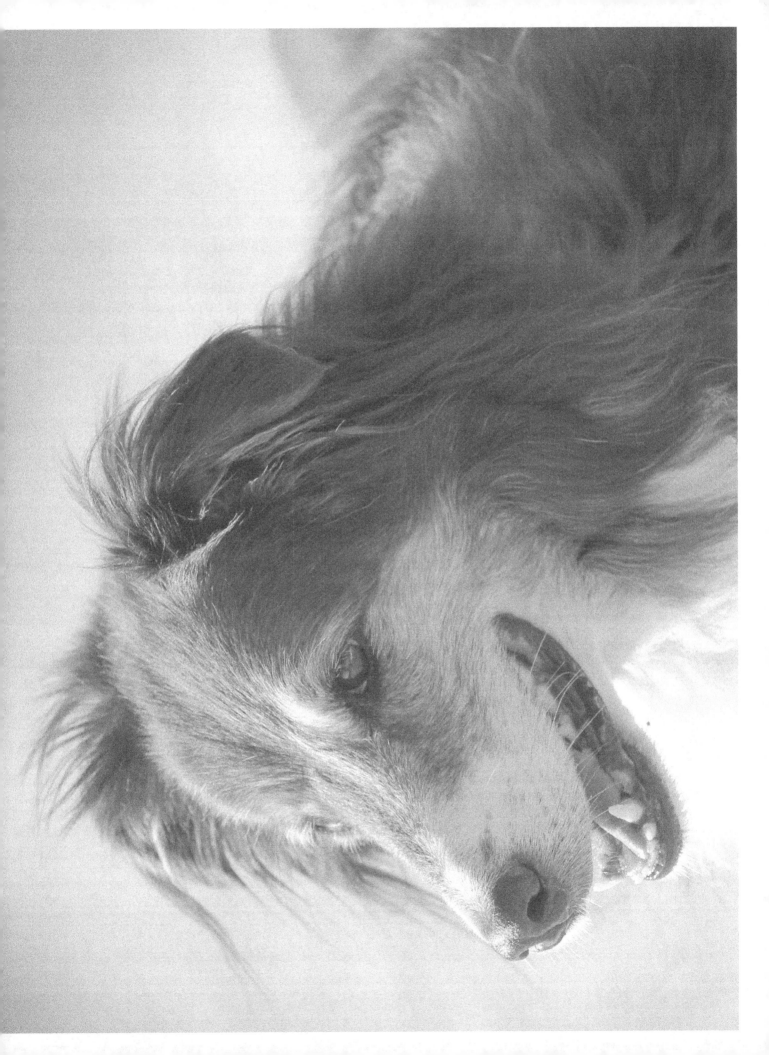

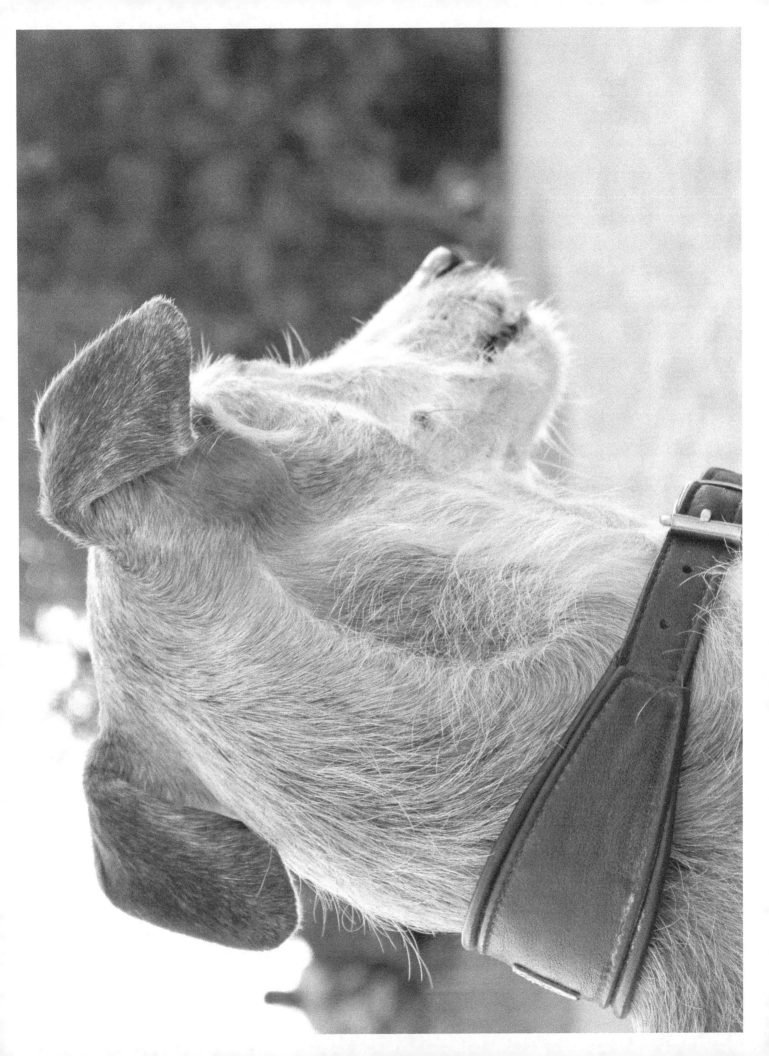

CPSIA information can be obtained
at www.ICGtesting.com
Printed in the USA
LVHW02s0351191217
560227LV00026B/1241/P